# BAD MEN

### HOW ADVERTISING WENT FROM A
### MINOR ANNOYANCE TO A MAJOR MENACE

## BOB HOFFMAN

**BadMen: How Advertising Went From A Minor Annoyance To A Major Menace**

by Bob Hoffman

Cover Design: Bonnie Miguel
Interior Design: Bonnie Miguel
Publisher: Type A Group, LLC
For information contact bob@typegroup.com

ISBN: 978-0-9992307-0-1

Also by
# BOB HOFFMAN

*Marketers Are From Mars, Consumers Are From New Jersey*

*101 Contrarian Ideas About Advertising*

*Quantum Advertising*

*The Ad Contrarian*

## About Bob

"FABULOUSLY IRREVERENT"
*Time, Inc*

"IF YOU DON'T KNOW WHO BOB HOFFMAN IS THEN YOU REALLY DON'T WORK IN ADVERTISING. THAT, OR YOU HAVE NOT STEEPED YOURSELF IN THE WISDOM OF THIS MAN."
*MediaPost*

"CAUSTIC YET TRUTHFUL"
*The Wall Street Journal*

"THE MOST PROVOCATIVE MAN IN ADVERTISING"
*Fuel Lines*

"SAVAGE CRITIQUES OF DIGITAL HYPE"
*Financial Times*

"IT'S NICE TO FIND A REAL THINKER IN THE AD BUSINESS THESE DAYS"
*Jack Trout, Forbes.com*

"BOB IS THE LITTLE CHILD WHO POINTS OUT THAT THE EMPEROR IS WEARING NO CLOTHES...I'M JEALOUS. I WISH I'D BEEN BRAVE ENOUGH TO BE THIS RUDE."
*Prof. Byron Sharp, author, "How Brands Grow"*

About *"Marketers Are From Mars,
Consumers Are From New Jersey"*

"A FUNNY AND UPROARIOUS READ"
Douglas Burnett, *"The Marketing Book Podcast"*

"HOFFMAN IS A VOICE OF REASON IN OUR INCREASINGLY
CRAZY WORLD OF ADVERTISING. HIS NO BULLSHIT, DOWN
TO EARTH INSIGHT WILL HAVE YOU QUESTIONING AND
REEXAMINING EVERYTHING YOU DO"
*MediaPost*

"LIKELY THE FUNNIEST MARKETING BOOK EVER"
*Amazon Review*

"THIS BOOK SHOULD BE REQUIRED READING AT EVERY
ADVERTISING SCHOOL IN THE COUNTRY"
Rich Siegel, Author, *"Round Seventeen and a Half"*

"FANTASTIC, BRUTAL AND VERY HONEST"
*Amazon Review*

"HILARIOUS, IRREVERENT AND INFORMATIVE"
*Amazon Review*

# Dedication

To the wonderful Maria who I have little doubt will never read this book.

# Contents

# Introduction

*"Today in the United States we have somewhere close to four or five thousand data points on every individual ... So we model the personality of every adult across the United States, some 230 million people."*

—*Alexander Nix (Chief Executive, Cambridge Analytica), October 2016.*

We were taught to fear totalitarian governments. We feared they would know everything about us, follow us everywhere, track our every move, and keep secret files about us which could be used to influence our lives in ways that were only vaguely visible to us.

We are well on our way to such a nightmare. Except it isn't our government that knows everything about us, follows us everywhere, tracks our every move, and keeps secret files about us. It is the marketing industry.

This book is about "surveillance marketing." Surveillance marketing is powered largely by advertisers through the tracking of our movements on the web. This is called "ad tech."

Advertisers used to use media to send information to us. Today they use media, specifically the web, to collect information about us. As Doc Searls says, online advertising is *"tracking-aimed junk mail that only looks like ads."*

This book is not meant to be an even-handed look at online advertising. I hate online advertising and I'm not ashamed to say it. I think it is unnecessarily crappy, corrupt and dangerous and is in desperate need of reform. This will not be a "fair and balanced" look at it. I am trying my very best to make it fair but imbalanced.

Someday someone will write a comprehensive and perhaps even-handed book on this subject. This isn't it. This is a small, hysterical book.

It's not just advertisers that are guilty. Google, Facebook, Amazon and other online media properties have created amazing stuff. The products they have created, the services they provide, and the technology they have given us are unprecedented and, sometimes, wonderful. But in the process they have also created an unnecessarily monstrous, mostly invisible, highly dangerous hidden world of information collection and distribution about us that is also unprecedented — and fraught with peril.

They have legions of stooges and suck-ups to tell you how wonderful their business practices are. This is the other side.

I'm trying to straddle a line. I want this book to be interesting and enlightening to advertising and marketing professionals, but I also want it to be accessible to civilians. To accomplish this, and to keep suicides to a minimum, I am intentionally omitting a lot of the horrifying language of marketing.

Finally, I want to apologize for the title. I stipulate that advertising is no longer a "mens' club" and that *BadMen* only covers half the landscape. But *BadMen and Women*, while technically a more accurate description of reality, is such a cringe-inducing title that I could not in good conscience inflict it on you.

Nonetheless, I am happy to acknowledge that in the advertising industry today women have proven themselves to be equally irresponsible to their male counterparts.

Kudos all around.

# Chapter One:

## Every Step You Take

*We used to have a pleasant enough arrangement with the ad industry. They gave us Seinfeld and in return we voluntarily gave a few seconds of our attention to their ads. It was a reasonably fair exchange.*

*Today, the ad industry gives us fake news, clickbait and cat videos and we involuntarily give them our names, addresses, health history, sexual predilections, banking information, psychological profiles, credit history, and dozens of other tidbits of personal information.*

*And they sell it to whomever the hell they please.*

## TIME TO GO

It was in 2011 that I knew I had to leave the advertising industry.

I was ceo of a pretty successful agency with offices in San Francisco and St Louis. We had high profile clients like McDonald's and Toyota. But I was getting a bad feeling about what was going on.

A year earlier I had written a piece for Adweek magazine called "Big Brother Has Arrived, And He's Us." It was about the dangers of online tracking. Here's what I wrote at the time:

*...The essence of freedom and democracy is being undermined. We can't see it, but it's all around us. It's that "fish can't see the ocean" thing. What's threatening our freedom is tracking on the Internet.*

*The Internet now knows everything about us. It knows where we go, who we talk to, what we talk about, what and who we like and don't like. It knows what we buy and why we buy it. It knows what we sell and who we sell it to. It knows our names, our addresses, our phone numbers, our credit card numbers, our bank and brokerage accounts. It knows how much money we have, where we keep it and what we do with it. It knows our location at any moment and whom we are with.*

*It knows our political beliefs and our sexual habits. It knows what we eat and whether we drink too much. It knows what we think of our bosses and what our bosses think of us. It knows our salaries and our payment histories. It knows what airlines we fly, what cars we buy and what hotels we stay at. It knows what our ailments are, what drugs we use, what doctors we see and what our psychological profiles are.*

*It relentlessly collects this information 24 hours a day, 365 days a year. It keeps this information in flimsy warehouses where anyone with time or ingenuity can find anything they want to know about us.*

*It pretends the information is secure, but only a blind fool believes this. It tells us that privacy is an old-fashioned, out-of-date concept. It is reassuring in its pervasiveness.*

*Then it sells the information to the highest bidder. And sometimes to any bidder at all. And why does it do all this? For us. For the marketing and advertising industries.*

*There's no reasonable way that this is a good development for a free society. There is no realistic vision of the future in which this will not lead to appalling mischief.*

*It's time for us to say no. It's time to put aside our petty self-interest, take a step back and see where this is leading. We need to stop tracking people and their behavior.*

*Big Brother has arrived, and he's us.*

But it wasn't just tracking, privacy and security that troubled me. Online advertising had turned me into a liar. The advertising industry is world famous for bullshit — a reputation that was honestly earned. But bullshit is different from lying. The realization came to me slowly. But one day it came hard.

I was in a meeting. We were presenting a Powerpoint deck to a client with the results of an online ad campaign.

Midway through the meeting we got to a slide with the click-through rate for the campaign. We had buried it nicely in a very complex table. We quickly went through the table and moved on to the next slide.

The client interrupted, *"Excuse me, can you go back one slide."* We held our breath and went back to the slide with the click rate – which was .02%

*"Two percent,"* the client said, *"that's not bad."*

Nobody said a word. Nobody said *".02% is not two percent. It's two hundredths of one percent. It's not two clicks in a hundred. It's two clicks in ten thousand."*

And we quickly moved on to the next slide.

I had just become a liar - no different from the online ad hustlers I had been railing against for years. I knew then that I had to leave the advertising industry. Soon thereafter (with a little unwelcome enthusiasm from some of my junior partners) I left the agency business. And I stopped lying.

Anyone in the agency business who's half awake has known for years that online display advertising is fraught with corruption and flimflam. As Forrester research recently wrote, *"Display advertising never worked like we pretended. CMOs know this but nobody wants to talk about it."*

We were afraid of the truth for a few reasons.

First was self-preservation. Anyone in an agency who questioned digital supremacy was immediately labeled a Luddite dinosaur, and was marked for extinction. Try telling ISIS you don't believe in their God. You'll soon be ten inches shorter.

It became clear that it was better to be *wrong* within the normal range than *right* outside the normal range. And the normal range required a belief in online advertising supremacy.

For example, a social media campaign your client was demanding may have been a monumental waste of time and money, but by expressing skepticism about it you fell outside the normal range and were in danger. You would be better off enthusiastically supporting it even if you knew it would fail miserably - as most do. By supporting it you would be in the normal range. By questioning it, you would be dangerously retro.

Clients hungered to believe in the online miracle. Agencies who told the truth soon found themselves losing long-held accounts to uber-trendy agencies with fast-talking hustlers equipped with a sackful of digital miracles.

That was a few years ago. The astounding part of all this is that even though the facts about online advertising have been uninspiring at best and shocking at worst, the bullshit continues. In some places, it's still perilous to say out loud that the emperor's wardrobe is insufficient.

We used to be able to pretend we didn't know. But these days we can't pretend we don't know. We know the facts about online advertising. But the truth remains dangerous, and the consequences remain daunting.

## MORPHING INTO A MONSTER

I'm a copywriter.

I don't know very much about technology. I also don't know very much about media buying or selling.

So why have I written a book about "ad tech?" Because although I don't know much about technology or media, I think I know a little something about bullshit.

I spent 41 years in the agency business. You think you're full of shit? I have a lifetime achievement award.

And I think some software people and some agency people have gotten together and sold the marketing industry a bunch of dangerous crap known as ad tech.

I believe that on the whole advertising and marketing people are good people. We are hard-working and well-meaning. We want to help our brands and our clients succeed. We want to make good products for consumers and provide them with good service.

If the realization came to us that something we're doing might be marginally beneficial to our company but was clearly harmful to consumers, clearly harmful to our industry, and clearly harmful to society, I would hope we would have the integrity to give it some serious scrutiny.

I'm afraid that is the situation we find ourselves in today.

It is hard for us to imagine that a technology we are using - that began with the simple and benign purpose of delivering online ads to websites - has morphed into a monster. We never intended it to be so. But it's time to face reality. Ad tech - as it is currently practiced - is a menace.

As *The New York Times* says,

> "We've come to understand that privacy is the currency of our online lives, paying for petty conveniences with bits of personal information.

*But we are blissfully ignorant of what that means. We don't know what data is being bought and sold, because, well, that's private. The evidence that flashes in front of our own eyes looks harmless enough: We search Google for a new pair of shoes, and for a time, sneakers follow us across the web, tempting us from every sidebar. But our information can also be used for matters of great public significance, in ways we're barely capable of imagining."*

*The Wall Street Journal* says,

*"Digital technology has become critical to the personal and economic well-being of everyone on the planet, but decisions about how it is designed, operated and developed have never been voted on by anyone. Those decisions are largely made by executives and engineers at Google, Facebook, Amazon and other leading tech companies, and imposed on the rest of us with very little regulatory scrutiny."*

The collection and exploitation of personal information for advertising purposes is part of what we in the ad industry call "ad tech." It also includes the use of software programs to buy, sell and distribute advertising on the web. It is powered by "tracking." Tracking is just a pleasanter word for surveillance - and it has led to all kinds of hazardous consequences.

- It is subverting our industry's relationship with the public.
- It has enabled a cesspool of corruption and an ocean of fraud.
- It places personal and private information about us within the reach of criminals, governments, and other potential malefactors.
- It has devalued the work of legitimate online publishers
- It is degrading our news media and journalism
- It is distrusted by marketers.

-     It is despised by the public.

Other than that, it's great.

.

     Let's review the facts.

- As a result of the public's disgust with online advertising, over 600 million web-connected devices are now armed with ad blockers. According to Doc Searls author of *The Cluetrain Manifesto* and *The Intention Economy*, this is the largest boycott of anything in the history of humanity.

- According to the World Federation of Advertisers (hereafter known as the WFA) by 2025 online ad fraud, enabled substantially by tracking, may become the second largest source of criminal income in the world

- Ad tech drives money to the worst online publishers. Ad tech's value proposition is this: we will find you the highest quality eyeballs at the cheapest possible locations. Ad tech can do this because your web browser and mobile platform are vulnerable to a problem called "data leakage" where your activity on a trusted site is revealed to other companies. Viewers developed by quality publishers like *The Washington Post* are tagged and followed to crappy websites like kittylittervideo.com and served ads there instead of at the *Post's* website.

- This has resulted in the struggle for existence among quality online publishers and has lead to the "brand safety" crisis marketers are currently struggling with. Ad tech algorithms automatically deliver their ads to cheap websites - sometimes run by terrorists, racists, and pornographers

- Dollars not driven to the shittiest possible locations are driven to Facebook and Google which some marketers think of as safe havens but are, in fact, an arrogant duopoly who have refused to abide by widely-accepted standards of measurement, openness and transparency. They are the key defenders and beneficiaries of tracking. They are in the surveillance business and are making billions doing it.

- Somewhere between 40% and 60% of "programmatic" (automated) ad budgets are being scraped by ad tech middlemen, depending on whose numbers you choose to believe.

- Ad agency holding companies have invested heavily in ad tech. There is suspicion that their enthusiasm for online advertising may be driven substantially by self-interest rather than the interests of their clients.

- Ad tech is also the economic engine behind fake news. One of its most pernicious effects is the corruption of journalism.

- And what has ad tech given us in return? An overall rate of effectiveness that is usually reported at about 6 clicks per 10,000 ads served. Solve Media says a person is more likely to complete Navy SEAL training than click on a banner ad.

- Finally, everything the ad tech industry has ever told us about privacy and security has, in the fullness of time, turned out to be complete horseshit. They are incompetent, irresponsible, and dangerous.

Technology is a trial and error endeavor. Nobody gets technology right the first time. The Wright brothers didn't, Thomas Edison didn't, Steve Jobs didn't. And guess what? The ad industry didn't either.

One of the positions that tracking apologists take is that if we opposed tracking and ad tech we are standing in the way of progress.

This is a profoundly misguided argument.

Technology is not synonymous with progress. Our ability to manage technology wisely determines if technology is progress or not. Even a cursory knowledge of history teaches us that we are at least as capable of using technology for evil as for good.

The idea that all types of technology constitute "progress" is dangerously shallow. The idea that opposing malevolent uses of technology impedes "progress" is irresponsibly stupid.

We are dealing with a very clear risk-reward situation here. The rewards of ad tech, if any, have been quite low. The risks have become enormous.

We don't need ad tech as it is currently configured.

We can do online advertising better, more successfully, and more profitably without spying on the public, destroying our credibility, enriching criminals, degrading our news media, and endangering our freedoms

## WHAT IS AD TECH?

Now that you know the thesis of this book, let's go back and be sure we understand the basics.

Ad tech started simply as an automated method for buying, selling, and distributing online advertising.

Online advertising is different from other forms of advertising in one very important way. In traditional advertising an advertiser buys advertising space from a publisher, like *The New York Times*. You buy a page in *The Times* for next Sunday, and you can see your ad right there in the newspaper next Sunday.

Online advertising is bought differently. You don't buy an ad unit, you buy a type of *person*. What ad tech does is track each of us around the web and delivers ads to us anywhere we go. So when you buy online advertising, you are *not* buying space in a publication and you often have no idea where on the web your ad may run.

The purported benefit to the advertiser is this. Instead of reaching Bob Hoffman by running your ad on *The New York Times* website, where it might cost $1 to reach Bob, you can follow him to b*ikinibeachbabes.com* a much lower quality website, where you can show him the same ad and it may cost you only a nickel.

In the real world, the online advertising supply chain is so replete with garbage that serving an ad to most websites costs tenths or even hundredths of a penny.

On the surface, the value proposition of ad tech - reaching the highest value eyeballs at the cheapest possible locations - is an appealing proposition. But as we shall see, advertising has probably never experienced a wider gap between theory and reality.

To get a feel for how complicated this whole thing has become, have a look at this chart

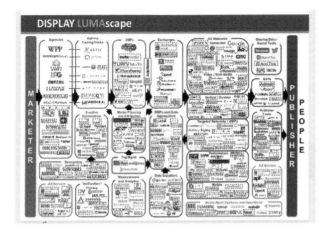

What you are looking at is a diagram called a "Lumascape" after *Luma* Partners, the investment firm that invented it. It represents the possible technological routes a progammatic ad buy can take to get from an advertiser to a website.

I will not try to describe these routes for the simple reason that they are essentially incomprehensible. The path from advertiser to publisher weaves its way through trading desks, DSPs (Demand Side Platforms), data providers, targeting programs, verification software, ad exchanges and an insane and murky gauntlet of other toll takers who each extract a little money from the advertiser's media budget. As we will see later, the amount of shrinkage along the way is shocking.

## THE DECEIVERS

Online advertising had a difficult birth. It started with a big fantasy. The fantasy was that people would want to interact with it.

We in the agency business were promised that online advertising would be far more effective than traditional advertising because it would be interactive. In fact, for many years it was called "interactive" advertising.

This fantasy lived for a while until reliable data arrived and it became clear that consumers had virtually no interest in interacting with online advertising. In fact, click rates (the only possible way to interact with online advertising) on banner ads were so low, companies like Facebook refused to divulge them.

The idea that the same person who was frantically clicking her tv remote to escape from advertising would gleefully click her mouse to interact with it is going to go down as one of the great marketing delusions of all time.

There are two ways online publishers make money - traffic and clicks. In light of the indifference consumers were demonstrating toward display advertising, publishers needed to find ways to generate sufficient traffic (visitors to a website) and/or clicks to attract advertisers and make money.

One of the strategies they evolved was to disguise advertising as something else.

When you see a TV commercial, a billboard or a magazine ad, there is no question what it is. It is an attempt to sell you something. It may be annoying, stupid, and tiresome, but there is no doubt about the nature of what it is or what its motives are. It is an ad and it wants to sell you something.

Online advertising is different. It has become devious, non-transparent, and unscrupulous. It is often intentionally confusing and its motives are often unclear. It does everything possible to hide its real intent.

Google earns most of its money by subtle misdirection. They have proven to be geniuses at it. Their search engine business is founded on the idea of misdirection – create a *paid* search result that seems to a consumer to be close enough to a *natural* search result to be believable. This is the essence of their business.

When you search for "Gloves" as I did here, you get an ad disguised as a search result.

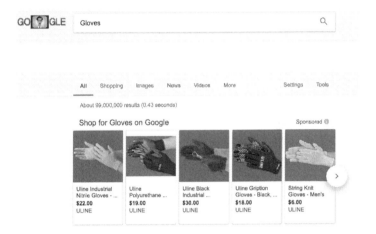

Unless you happen to notice the word "sponsored" in the upper right corner, and happen to know that by "sponsored" Google means "this is an ad" you would believe you're getting a search result.

In many cases, Google has made a minimal attempt to identify ads by including a little "ad" badge on paid results. But the overall look and feel of the ads is so similar to search results that according to independent research half of people can't distinguish between an ad and a search result. There is only one possible explanation for this - Google is intentionally blurring the lines.

This is not the only way Google strives to deceive. According to *The Wall Street Journal*, the Federal Trade Commission has reported

"... *Google Inc. manipulated search results to favor its own services over rivals', even when they weren't most relevant for users...the*

*FTC's bureau of competition found evidence that Google boosted its own services for shopping, travel and local businesses by altering its ranking criteria and "scraping" content from other sites. It also deliberately demoted rivals."*

The *Journal* also recently reported that

*"...ads for products sold by Google and its sister companies appeared in the most prominent spot in 91% of 25,000 recent searches related to such items...*

*The results show how Google uses its dominant search engine to boost other parts of its business and give it an edge over competitors....After the Journal shared the analysis with Google on Dec. 15, many of the ads disappeared ...Google declined to comment on the disparity."*

Recently, Google was issued the largest fine in history by the EU — $2.7 billion — for illegally favoring search results for its own businesses.

Here's an illustration from *The Wall Street Journal*...

**Steering Customers**
European regulators accuse Google of unfairly favoring its shopping ads in search results, while Google says they are good for users.

Yahoo is in the top 5 websites in the U.S. by visitor count. Here is a a screen grab from this morning's (as I write this) front page news feed.

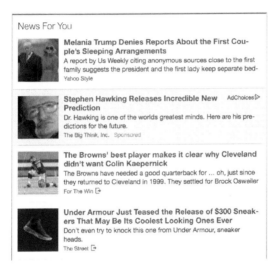

Let's ignore for a second the unspeakable crap that Yahoo considers front page news. One of the leading stories on this front page is not a news story at all. It is an ad disguised as a news story (it's the Stephen Hawking story.)

Facebook uses the names of its users to create phony testimonial ads which falsely imply that your friends and family are endorsing the brands in question. This practice amounts to hijacking user identities and disguising them as product endorsements. The ad below appeared in my Facebook feed.

The ad mentions Lucy Hoffman and Dallas Baker and implies that they are endorsers of the offer. In fact they are not. I know this because Lucy Hoffman is my daughter and Dallas Baker, a former business colleague, is a fanatical fan of the San Francisco Giants.

Below is another example.

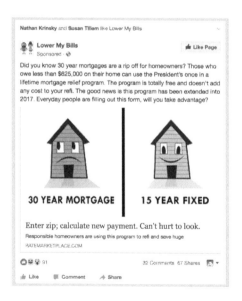

I have contacted both Nathan Krinsky and Susan Tillem, the people referenced in the ad, and have confirmed that neither of them knew they were being used in this way.

When Mr. Krinsky was questioned about this his response was, "how did they get my name?" He said he had no awareness of their using his name. He did not give permission and he did not "like" that advertiser.

Actually, he did give permission but didn't know it. The permission for Facebook to engage in this deceptive practice is buried deep in the agreement we sign when we open a Facebook account.

There is only one explanation for this – Facebook is intentionally exploiting a legal loophole to deceive us into thinking our friends are endorsing products and brands which they are not endorsing.

Many of the ads in my current Facebook feed are identified as "suggested posts." I wonder what language it is in which "suggested post" means "ad?" As usual, online advertising is doing its best to confuse what is an ad and what is not.

Social Media may be the most egregious corrupter of reasonable advertising standards. Its tricks have included: fraudulent reviews, spamming with dishonest tweets from non-existing people, propagation and distribution of fake news.

One of the most dangerous outcomes of this has been the corruption of the news industry.

The ability of fake news to make money for its creators is enabled mainly by ad tech. In very simple terms, a fake news story (generally lead by a "clickbait" headline) runs on a social media platform, attracts traffic and clicks, which signals programmatic systems to buy advertising on the site. Below is an egregious example of a successful fake news story.

Since our recent presidential campaign "fake news" has been a big story. It is nothing new, as this wonderful front page from the *Weekly World News* of 2002 shows. But this time around it's a lot more serious.

The narrative during the presidential election went something like this: fake news is the result of a desire by partisan operatives to gain political advantage. There is certainly no shortage of bullshit emanating from partisan operatives, and Facebook has acknowledged that it was used to propagate fake political news. But I believe fake news is at least as attributable to easy ad tech money as it is to politics.

The arcane and impossibly convoluted nature of the online ad business has made the publication and monetization of fake news on sleazy websites a very easy way to pick up some decent pocket change. Teenagers and others with no political motives have learned how easy it is put up a website, load it with stolen or invented "content", promote it on social media, and wait for the ads and money to roll in.

When "programmatic" algorithms see that people (or bots) are going to these sites, they send ads. Whose ads? If you're an advertiser, yours. Whose money supports this fake news? Yours.

A second corruption of journalism is the development and acceptance of "native advertising" as a legitimate form of commercial discourse. Despite its euphemistically lovely name, native advertising is nothing but advertising disguised as news.

Legitimate news organizations, desperate to make money at all costs, have been forced into agreeing to run thinly disguised advertising pieces masquerading as news or content. The rot has gotten so deep that some once-reputable news organizations have actually set up studios for the creation of this stuff, and are going so far as to oversee its wide dissemination on social media channels on behalf of its clients.

In the item below, an ad for Toyota is sprinkled among editorial content in *The New York Times* T Magazine.

**More in T Magazine**                                      Go to the T Magazine Section »

**7 Key Themes in Rei Kawakubo's Career**

**The Photographer Who Captured People Driving in Los Angeles**

PAID POST: **TOYOTA**
U.S. Army Soldiers Wear These Boots to Lighten Their Load

**A Spring Picnic Recipe From Two Rising N.Y.C. Chefs**

ON THE VERGE
**Brand to Know: The Kenyan Line That Makes Only One Dress**

**Men's Fashion: 8 Things Every Guy Can Wear This Spring**

It's hard to overestimate the damage that ad tech has had on the credibility of our news media. The fact that we have a populace that no longer knows what to believe from a media industry they once trusted is not an accident.

# Chapter Two:
## Every Move You Make

In 2014, Yahoo's chief of security went to the ceo and the board of directors to recommend changes. He was afraid that their millions of subscribers were at risk because of holes in Yahoo's security.

He recommended that they adopt full encryption that would make their platform far more secure.

But the person who ran their email and messaging services objected. According to The New York Times, he claimed "...it would have hurt Yahoo's ability to index and search message data..."

What that means is that Yahoo would not be able to scan our emails and text messages and use the information gleaned from doing so to create targeting opportunities for their advertising clients.

The ceo and the board rejected the recommendation of the security chief.

Soon thereafter, 500 million Yahoo accounts were hacked.

## TRACKING AND PRIVACY

In June of 2013, the snot hit the fan when *The Washington Post* and *The Guardian* reported that the US had secret spying programs that were *"tapping directly into the central servers of nine leading U.S. Internet companies."*

It was inevitable that our industry's obsession with data collection would come smack up against questions of civil liberties and individual rights. But very few in the marketing or advertising industries seemed to care about the consequences of our obsession with data, or the central role we were playing in this controversy.

It is an article of faith in the marketing community that the internet has given us reg'lar folks more control over our lives. One of the mantras of marketing's chattering class is that *"the consumer is in charge."*

The hypothesis behind this is the belief that traditionally power has been in the hands of marketers. But today, because of the internet, the consumer has the power.

Underlying this is the viewpoint that the internet has had a democratizing effect that is good for consumers and good for society. The thinking is that it has given the individual more power and more control. I am not so sure. In fact, I am highly skeptical.

If the Internet has produced any change in the power relationship between consumers and marketers, it may very well be in favor of the marketers. The amount of information they are collecting, warehousing, and selling about us is outrageous and alarming.

From *The Wall Street Journal...*

> *"Some of the most widely used apps on Facebook—the games, quizzes and sharing services that define the social-networking site and give it such appeal—are gathering volumes of personal information.*

> *A Wall Street Journal examination of 100 of the most popular*

*Facebook apps found that some seek the email addresses, current location and sexual preference, among other details, not only of app users but also of their Facebook friends. One Yahoo service powered by Facebook requests access to a person's religious and political leanings as a condition for using it. The popular Skype service for making online phone calls seeks the Facebook photos and birthdays of its users and their friends...a user's friends aren't notified if information about them is used by a friend's app. An examination of the apps' activities also suggests that Facebook occasionally isn't enforcing its own rules on data privacy."*

The idea that the consumer is in charge is a mirage. People think that because they can tweet *"the fries at Wendy's really suck"* we now have greater economic, social and political control. They are alarmingly blind to the trade-offs the web has presented us with.

The illusion that we are in charge is masking the fact that the powerful are getting more powerful and that the individual citizen has less control than ever. You have to be mighty naive to believe that *they* have all the information but *we* are in charge.

Whether the benefit our government is getting from all this surveillance is worth the price we are paying in civil liberties is above the pay grade of an ad writer. But the issue of marketing's role in all this is not.

Governments have always concocted reasonable sounding excuses for spying on their citizens. There has never been a time when there wasn't some "threat to public safety" that articulate leaders couldn't twist into a rationale for a secret branch of government. The difference now is, we in the advertising/marketing/media complex are complicit.

***

One thing we have learned is that we can never accept at face value anything anyone associated with web privacy tells us.

Marketers tell us that the information they collect is anonymous. As usual, this is baloney.

On July 7, 2017, *The Wall Street Journal* reported:

> *"...modern data-analysis tools are capable of finding links between large databases...*
>
> *Two years ago, researchers at the Massachusetts Institute of Technology discovered shoppers could be identified by linking social-media accounts to anonymous credit-card records and bits of secondary information, such as the location or timing of purchases.*
>
> *'I don't think people are aware of how easy it is getting to de-anonymize data,' said Ishaan Nerurkar, whose startup LeapYear Technologies Inc. sells software for leveraging machine learning..."*

A piece in *The New York Times* revealed that most web privacy policies are complete bullshit. *The Times* did a study of the top 100 sites in the U.S. Here's what they discovered:

> *"Of the 99 sites with English-language terms of service or privacy policies, 85 said they might transfer users' information if a merger, acquisition, bankruptcy, asset sale or other transaction occurred"*

Or as the Assistant Attorney General of Texas put it...

> *"...we are never going to sell your data, except if we need to."*

The Executive Director of the Electronic Privacy Information Center had this to say...

> *"...companies make representations that are weak and provide little actual privacy protection to consumers."*

The hypocrisy of Silicon Valley aristocrats is breathtaking. Soon after the Edward Snowden affair, people who have made billions of dollars by collecting ungodly amounts of personal information about us came out in force to denounce governments for collecting ungodly amounts of personal information about us.

Here is an "Open Letter" they published in national newspapers.

# Global Government Surveillance Reform

The undersigned companies believe that it is time for the world's governments to address the practices and laws regulating government surveillance of individuals and access to their information.

While the undersigned companies understand that governments need to take action to protect their citizens' safety and security, we strongly believe that current laws and practices need to be reformed.

Consistent with established global norms of free expression and privacy and with the goals of ensuring that government law enforcement and intelligence efforts are rule-bound, narrowly tailored, transparent, and subject to oversight, we hereby call on governments to endorse the following principles and enact reforms that would put these principles into action.

They're shocked – shocked I tell you! – at the intrusion into our privacy. Except when they can make some money from it.

Recently, a coalition of advertising, marketing, and media trade associations joined the Trump administration in calling for the rejection of an FCC regulation created to protect consumers by restricting the collection and sharing of personal information by internet service providers like Comcast, Verizon, and AT&T.

The regulation would have given consumers far more control over their personal information by requiring them to opt-in before the ISPs (internet service providers) could collect or sell their personal information. The actions of the advertising industry in this instance are deplorable – but hardly surprising.

Jonathan Schwantes of the Consumers Union said, *"Consumers deserve to know—and have a say in—who is collecting certain information about them and how it's used."*

Listen to this crap from the 4A's, AAF, ANA, DMA and IAB* in defending this practice.

> *"Without prompt action in Congress or at the FCC, the FCC's regulations would break with well-accepted and functioning industry practices, chilling innovation and hurting the consumers the regulation was supposed to protect."*

Well-accepted practices like stalking us, selling our personal information to the highest bidder, enabling creeps and criminals to hack info about us. No, we wouldn't want to deprive them of innovations like that.

*American Association of Advertising Agencies; American Advertising Federation; Association of National Advertisers; Data & Marketing Association; Interactive Advertising Bureau.

## TRACKING AND FRAUD

According to the World Federation of Advertisers by 2025 ad fraud may be the second largest source of criminal income on the planet, after drug trafficking.

This is not good.

Dr. Augustine Fou, an expert on ad fraud, says there are basically two types of ad fraud: traffic fraud and click fraud.

Both traffic and click fraud are primarily due to bots (or robotic software threads) pretending to be humans. Some ad fraud is human in nature with "click farms" full of people who make money by doing nothing all day but sitting around and clicking on websites and ads. But bots are the bigger problem.

Most advertisers pay for online ad space on the basis of how much traffic a site delivers to them or how many clicks it delivers. In other words, traffic and clicks are the basic currency of online economics.

What most advertisers don't understand is that the reports they get on traffic and clicks are often false. These reports contend that visitors are real but they are not. As the WFA says, *"...reporting validates a visitor to be authentic, but it is actually fraudulent."* Advertisers have no choice but to rely on these questionable reports because there is no other option. Believing these reports is like believing your 16-year-old's explanation of how the fender got dented.

One of the most difficult problems for advertisers to come to terms with is the size of online ad fraud. Everyone knows it's a headache, but no one knows what kind of headache. Is it just eye strain or am I having a stroke?

- Group M, a WPP-owned media company, says that ad fraud is "significantly contained" and that "2% of impressions purchased by the biggest advertisers in Western markets remain non-human."

- The&Partnership, another WPP-owned company, says that
  ad fraud was actually about $12.5b in that same year. So two
  divisions of the same company disagree on ad fraud's penetration
  by a margin of 1,000%.

- The Association of National Advertisers, on the other hand,
  claims that about $7.2 billion was stolen in 2016 by online ad
  fraudsters, which would amount to about 11% of total ad spend.

- Meanwhile, the World Federation of Advertisers says that
  fraud could be as high as $30 billion.

- In 2016 Facebook announced that they had cancelled a buying
  platform they were testing when they found that 75% of the
  inventory coming into the platform was "valueless."

- Oxford BioChronometrics, a cyber-security firm in the UK,
  says fraud can sometimes be as high as 90%.

In other words, everyone has an opinion and no one has a clue. Most
of the people I talk to who seem to be knowledgeable and reputable
guess that the number is between 10% and 40%. But the problem is, no
one really knows.

The difficulty in ascertaining a real number is that the people who
measure fraud (the cyber-security crowd) all have different criteria for
deciding whether a visitor is a human or a bot.

The security people have set up filters that look for patterns and try
to interpret what's a human pattern and what's a robotic pattern.

Meanwhile, the bad guys are constantly sending feelers to see which
patterns they can invent that will pass through the filters. Once they find
a winning pattern that will clear the filter, they bombard the system with
fraudulent traffic and clicks.

Consequently, when a cyber-security firm reports that only 5% of traffic is fraudulent, what they are really saying is that their nets were able to catch 5% of the fish, but they don't really know how many fish got through the nets.

In one instance, as a test, an ad fraud investigator sent 100% fraudulent traffic through an ad network and only 17% of it was identified as such by a leading cyber security firm.

Ad fraud carries with it almost no risk. According to Hewlett-Packard Enterprises, ad fraud has a higher payout potential and lower risk factor than any other type of online crime.

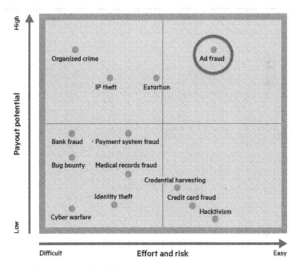

*Source: Hewlett-Packard Enterprises*

The scary part is that according to knowledgeable people, organized crime is not yet a major player in ad fraud. With so much money there for the taking, it is only a matter of time.

## WHY AD FRAUD THRIVES

If you're like me, you probably wonder how ad fraud can be so pervasive and harmful while the ad industry – with billions of dollars at stake
– sits on its fat ass and does nothing. The *aha!* moment came to me a
while back when I came across the chart below. It comes from the *World
Federation of Advertisers* and it explains a lot.

**THE AD FRAUD MONEY-FLOW:** COUNTING THE COST THROUGH THE CHAIN

SOURCE: WORLD FEDERATION OF ADVERTISERS,
*Compendium Of Ad Fraud Knowledge For Media Investors*

What this chart shows is that the flow of money within the ad tech
"ecosystem" is exactly the same whether agencies are buying real traffic
and real clicks or fraudulent traffic and fraudulent clicks.

The fraud doesn't enter the money stream until we get to the end,
by which time the people in the ad tech world have already cashed their
checks and are halfway to The Hamptons.

We might assume that the big gainers from online ad fraud are the
criminals themselves. But according to the WFA, the group that gains
the most is actually the legitimate marketing and advertising industry.
The more skin an ad agency or agency holding company has in the
ad tech money-flow chain (e.g., agency of record; trading desk; DSP;

ad tech provider, etc) the greater is its potential for revenue derived indirectly from ad fraud. In fact, as far as agencies and other marketing entities are concerned, fraud seems to add to their revenue stream.

This is not to say that agencies or marketing companies are complicit in ad fraud, but it is to say that they are inadvertently some of its biggest beneficiaries.

There are two groups of people getting royally screwed by ad fraud. First is asleep-at-the-wheel advertisers who astoundingly are still buying the hogwash they hear from their agencies about "systems they have in place" to identify and prevent ad fraud. You'd think that with all the recent headlines about ad fraud they'd start to connect the dots. But like all suckers, they always think it's *the other guy* who's getting screwed.

Second is online publishers. Advertisers are lining up to give their money to Google and Facebook and could not give less of a shit about the billion other online publishers out there. In fact, take away Google and Facebook and digital advertising is actually not growing.

This is dumping the significant problems of tracking and fraud on quality publishers. They are competing with fraudulent and junk sites for ad revenue, which drives prices down. And doubly hurtful is that the supply of fraudulent impressions is created from user data that is collected from their legitimate sites.

As a legitimate publisher you're in a double bind. You want to move advertisers from the "generic eyeball" market to quality sites where site reputation, not sneaky tracking, is the critical advantage. At the same time you have to play the existing game where you can't sell an ad unless you agree to infest your site with trackers that are data-leaking your user data to the junk sites you're competing with.

The gullibility of advertisers is beyond explanation. I can understand how they won't listen to half-wit bloggers like me, but how can they continue to ignore the overwhelming amount of evidence that is coming at them daily that shows they are being fucked blind?

I guess they must think there is someone somewhere who's looking after their interests. There isn't.

Their agencies aren't protecting them. It's not that agencies are complicit in the fraud, it's just that as the chart above shows, they have very little incentive to do anything about it. As long as clients keep pressing them for lower and lower media costs they'll continue to use programmatic methods for buying crappier and crappier crap.

Their CMOs aren't protecting them. It's largely these people who've been ramming digital fantasies down their throats for a decade.

The 4A's *(American Association of Advertising Agencies)* isn't protecting them. The 4A's has become the lapdog for the big 6 holding companies, and the big 6 are feasting at the online buffet. According to reports, as much as 40% of their income may be coming from online advertising.

The IAB *(Interactive Advertising Bureau)* is a cruel joke.

The ANA *(Association of National Advertisers)* seems to know they're getting screwed but have no idea what to do about it other than issue whiny press releases.

So who's going to protect dazed and confused marketers from themselves? To understand this better, let's take a brief detour and talk about basketball and hockey.

Basketball is a game with rules that greatly favor offense over defense. If you're playing defense and you breathe too hard on your opponent you're called for a foul. Consequently, basketball is a game with a lot of offense. You usually have to score over 100 points to win.

Hockey is the opposite. In hockey, the defensive player has some substantial advantages. You can pretty much maim or kill your opponent, as long as you don't do it with a high stick, and not be penalized. The result is that 3 goals are often enough to win a game.

In ad fraud, all the advantage is to the offense – that is, the fraudsters.

Fraudsters have tremendous incentive to be aggressive. They can make large amounts of money. What incentives do agencies, ad tech companies, or the 4A's have to play defense? Are they going to make more money? No. As we saw, it may even cost them money. So while the fraudsters are highly motivated to innovate, the defenders are slogging away dejectedly at what Rich Siegel calls "the long table of mediocrity."

The only people with an incentive to play defense are 1) the advertisers, who still don't understand the connection between demanding the lowest possible rates and getting the worst possible crap, and 2) the publishers, many of whom can only make a living by feeding advertisers "non-human" traffic (bots.)

One can only wonder how much more assiduously ad fraud remediation would be pursued if the unintentional beneficiaries were being punished instead of rewarded.

Oddly, not all ad fraud is revenue producing. In addition to all the crooks stealing billions, there are also malicious hackers just out to make trouble.

Ad agencies have been particularly negligent in educating their clients about how much they may be losing to ad fraud. Online advertising spending has surpassed TV. No one wants to disturb that golden goose. Meanwhile advertisers, seduced by the unrelenting hype about the miracle of online advertising can't get enough of the stuff.

## TRACKING AND TERRORISM

On Feb. 9, 2017 *The Times of London* ran a front page story about how major marketers were contributing to terrorists, racists and pornographers by inadvertently advertising on their websites.

It was well-known to anyone who cared to know that this was a problem for a long time. I discussed it on my blog years before *The Times* story. But *The Times* story was a tipping point. The story mentioned Disney, Honda, Mercedes-Benz and several other major brands whose advertising, had been running on horrible websites.

*The Times* also reported that these ads were running as pre-roll on *YouTube* for videos *"created by supporters of terrorist groups such as Islamic State and Combat 18, a violent pro-Nazi faction."*

A spokesperson for Google, which owns YouTube, said it had a *"zero-tolerance policy for content that incites violence or hatred."* Wow. Zero tolerance. I'm impressed! Except later that same day Fox News reported that it had found spots for Snickers, Budweiser, Hyundai and other advertisers running as pre-roll on jihadist videos on YouTube. So much for zero tolerance.

This set off a worldwide backlash against the threat to "brand safety" that online advertising was posing.

Over 250 advertisers, disgusted with the possibility of finding their advertising on extremist websites or alongside extremist videos, soon cancelled their advertising on the above-mentioned platforms. Here in the US, brands that cancelled included AT&T, Verizon, and J&J.

Almost two weeks after the scandal broke *The Wall Street Journal* reported in a front page story that it had *still* found major brand advertising all over extremist websites.

*"A Journal reporter, checking YouTube videos peddling conspiracies and racist views over the course of about five hours Thursday evening, found ads from major brands running on about 20 videos filled with racial slurs, hateful titles…"*

The Journal published this example of a Toyota ad on an anti-semitic video appearing on YouTube.

As a result of the Journal's findings Coke, Pepsi, Walmart, Starbuck's and others said they, too, were pulling their advertising from some or all of Google's properties.

The Journal said, *"the ease with which journalists have been able to find top brands' ads on controversial videos suggests Google is still failing to catch some of the most obvious examples."*

Google did a terrible job on two fronts. First they seemed unable to do anything about controlling this fire. Second, they looked like con men by trying to bullshit their customers – an executive at one of the affected advertisers said Google *"had assured us over the past few days that our brands were safe from this type of content..."*

On the broader front, the problem is not Google *per se*. Ad tech's promise of finding the most valuable eyeballs at the lowest cost locations cannot help but deliver advertising to appalling places.

So long as online advertising is locked into the current tracking model this will continue to be a headache for online advertisers. YouTube took the hit because that's where reporters went looking. But the problem is systemic

## KICKIN' BACK

On March 5, 2016 Jon Mandel, former CEO of Mediacom told an audience at the Association of National Advertisers (ANA) Media Leadership Conference about widespread U.S. agency kickbacks. He presented a document which purported to show how some of the kickbacks worked...

> *"...a media agency agreeing with an unnamed media vendor to an industry-standard 2% commission, but as much as 9% in volume-based incentives." (Ad Age)*

Since then, reports of kickbacks have appeared in *The Wall Street Journal*, and several other venues including a front page story in *Ad Age*, that reported...

> *"'It's really ugly and crooked,' said one ad-tech executive who described receiving such requests."*

> *"'It's the reason I left,' said a former U.S. media-agency executive."*

*Ad Age* reported,

> *"U.S.-based marketers are being kept out of the loop about billions of dollars that agencies make back from deals on clients' behalf, according to industry executives, whether in the form of opaque markups, kickbacks or undisclosed rebates."*

I seriously doubt the number is in the billions, but as we'll soon see, nobody knows.

Mandel said,

*"Have you ever wondered why fees to agencies have gone down and yet the declared profits to these agencies are up?"*

According to *The Wall Street Journal...*

*"Marketers say they're increasingly worried agencies are allocating ad dollars in ways that best suit their own businesses, as opposed to those of their clients."*

Brian Wieser, Senior Research Analyst at *Pivotal Research Group* said...

*"...most of the activity involving undisclosed activities is likely concentrated in digital."*

As a result of the revelations, the ANA teamed up with the 4As and decided to create a "Joint Task Force" to develop guidelines for media buying transparency. Presumably, this hoped-for transparency would allow the advertisers to fully understand exactly how their agencies were spending their money on media buys.

A "Joint Task Force," by the way, is the non-governmental equivalent of a "Blue Ribbon Panel." In other words, a bunch of overfed blowhards who get together at golf resorts to sip white wine and nap.

Well, to no one's surprise, the advertisers' definition of transparency was somewhat different from the agencys'. The advertisers' definition was "open up that kimono and let us see what's going on down there." The agencies' definition was "fuck you."

So, sadly, the Joint Task Force turned out to be a few seeds short of a joint.

Next thing you know, the ANA announced they were hiring not one, but two investigative organizations to look into the buying practices of agencies. And one of the organizations employed former FBI agents. As you might well imagine, this lead to severely diminished bowel control among several agency fat cats.

Now we cut to scene two.

Trying to preempt the ANA investigation, and without consulting them, the 4A's issued something called the *"Transparency Guiding Principles of Conduct"* which sounds like a chapter out of the Girl Scout manual. These guidelines pay solemn tribute to the concept of transparency while establishing it as essentially "whatever the hell we can sneak past your lawyers."

To which the ANA responded thusly: In quintessential Gestapo fashion they announced the opening of a snitch hotline in which any sniveling malcontent with a gripe against an agency could call in with anonymous accusations.

According to the Financial Times, the ANA's investigation was intended to...

> *"...probe the "non-transparent behaviour" of rebates, barter, arbitrage, dark pools, inventory management, global transactions, and supply chain media management."*

This is just corporate fancy talk for kickbacks and undisclosed fees.

According to *The Wall Street Journal*, a study done by *Forrester Research* and the ANA last year that interviewed high level marketing executives found that...

> *"...more than half of those polled noted a high level of concern over the possibility that agencies may receive a rebate from the media seller."*

Ad Age reported that the ANA's ceo said the effort would go beyond rebates and include arbitrage of digital ad inventory. What arbitrage means is that agencies buy ad space at one price and then resell it to their clients at another price. Except the clients don't know it. And guess what? The price the agencies sell it at is higher than the price they buy it at. Who'd a thunk it?

After about six months, the ANA released its report on transparency. It was a disgrace.

It's hard to imagine that there has ever been a report on transparency that was less transparent. It tarnished everyone in general and no one in particular. It reached conclusions that were reached by anyone with a functioning brain years ago.

The ANA interviewed about 150 people in and around the media/agency/client world and came up with conclusions you could have reached interviewing three puppy dogs and a salami sandwich.

Here's what we learned:

-Ad tech has been a black box for clients and a lovely source of money for agencies.

- Dirty dealing is *"pervasive"*

- Clients have absolutely no idea what they're doing. The people who are supposed to know what's going on (the CMOs) don't. This is news? To whom?

- Client procurement departments are accomplishing the exact opposite of their intended effect. The more they're trying to screw agencies the more they're getting screwed in return.

- *"Five of the six major agency holding companies...declined formal requests to make any of their current executives available to be interviewed."* Which is really everything you need to know

Here's what the report failed to do:

- Give us specific examples of who did what to whom. Without specifics, everyone's a suspect and no one's a crook.

- Give us any idea what the comparative levels of corruption are in different media. They went out of their way a number of times to protect the online industry by stating that the dirty dealings are not limited to online. But it was obvious from the language and the examples that the web is the muy grande cesspool of corruption.

There is no one who has been more critical of agency buying practices over the years than I have. I called for an investigation years ago. In a post called *"Time To Clean Out The Stables"* I wrote…

*"This industry is in desperate need of investigation."*

But this "investigation" was pathetic. It didn't name names. It didn't follow the money. It didn't provide any specifics. It just gave us "he said/she said," which was great ammo for guilty agencies to shoot back at the ANA. It was worse than a whitewash. It was a blackwash. It tainted everyone and accused no one.

Then we had the 4A's reaction. The less said about this witless nonsense the better. If you wanted to create a playbook of how guilty parties obfuscate and throw smoke in your face, you couldn't have done a better job. It was a text book example of how to torture language to be unmistakably devious and unconvincing.

Ultimately, agencies bought their way out of this mess

According to *Business Insider*, the big agencies proved their "innocence" by paying out millions to aggrieved advertisers. According to *Business Insider's* report, there have been at least 20 cases in which secret payments have been made or were being negotiated. Advertisers are getting as much as $10 million and more in recompense from "innocent" agencies for their charming media buying habits – *"particularly digital media."*

It was a critical moment for the 4A's and they blew it.

They lost any credibility about the innocence of their members by standing by while they made secret payoffs. The 4A's needed to investigate the *Business Insider* story and let us know of it was true. If the story was correct, the leaders of the 4A's either should have withdrawn their previous denials or stepped down. They should not have been allowed to squander the remains of the credibility of the ad industry in a misguided effort to defend a gaggle of unsavory aristocrats.

The ANA was not blameless in this either. In order to get their hush money, the advertisers had to agree to auction off their virtue:

1. They had to agree *not to audit* the agencies.

2. They had to agree *not to require the agencies to reveal the secret contracts* they had with media suppliers.

3. They had to *sign a non-disclosure agreement* in which they promised never to reveal that they traded integrity for money.

In other words, they agreed to leave the door open for more underhanded practices by not bringing to light what has been happening. Now every advertiser has to *guess* what shady deals have been going on and guess where the loopholes may be in their agency agreements. If the ANA had any sense, for their own self-interest, they'd pressure their members to lay all the cards on the table.

The payoffs have been carefully kept *"below the materiality threshold at which agency holding companies would have to disclose them in their annual reports."* Isn't that lovely? When is the SEC going to have a nice close look at these cutie pies?

### ANOTHER DAY, ANOTHER SCANDAL

November of 2016 two major scandals hit the online advertising business, adding to the litany of unscrupulous practices that are its norm.

First, it was discovered that for *two years* Facebook had been reporting a grossly inflated measure of the time people spent watching videos on Facebook's site – inflating their numbers by as much as 80%. (How screwed up do you have to be to be off by 80%? Well, I'm eleven feet tall, so I know!)

Of course, the extent of the baloney had to be dragged out of the people at Facebook. At first, without making any kind of serious announcement, they tried to sneak it by us on a post in their *"Advertiser Help Center"* by saying they had merely "renamed a metric." Yeah, by the way, I didn't steal your home, I just renamed the owner

Kudos to *Publicis* for seeing through this horseshit, digging their heels in and insisting that Facebook reveal the true nature of their game. Or at least the visible part of it.

Remember, like Google, Facebook *refuses to accept industry standards*. They haven't allowed impartial third parties to fully audit their numbers. Regardless of their excuses, there was only one logical explanation for these guys not allowing full third party auditing – because their numbers must have been bullshit. Well, now we *know* they were bullshit.

The second scandal involved Dentsu, the world's 5th largest agency network.

Dentsu has an astounding stranglehold on every aspect of media and marketing in Japan. According to the *Financial Times*, Dentsu has an

> *"...empire of advertising agencies, brand consultancies and public relations subsidiaries includes ties with TV broadcasters and Japan's two biggest news agencies — a network of influence that stretches deeply into corporate and public life."*

In other words, their power and influence in Japanese media are totally out of control. In recent years Dentsu has been extending its reach worldwide through the acquisition of Aegis, a global media buyer, and other non-Japanese companies.

After being hounded by one of its biggest clients (Toyota) Dentsu finally admitted that for *about 5 years* they had been guilty of screwing clients out of millions by engaging in online buying trickery. As the scandal grew, over 600 cases involving over 100 Dentsu clients were being investigated.

Meanwhile, here in the U.S., G.E., J.P. Morgan Chase, and Nationwide Insurance have launched audits of their agencies. One can only wonder when other U.S. companies will wake up and look into how vigorously they're being penetrated by the con men relentlessly hustling the miracle of online advertising at them.

The ad industry has never seen anything like the crookedness and sleaze of online advertising. And I have never seen anything like the willful ignorance and gullibility of today's "marketing and advertising professionals."

## LIFE AMONG THE OLIGARCHS

It wasn't long ago that digital utopians labeled the web the "information superhighway" and, as we've seen, promoted it as the great democratizing medium that would give us all a voice.

For a good laugh, here's a quote from Arianna Huffington from 2012…

> *"Thanks to YouTube – and blogging and instant fact-checking and viral emails – it is getting harder and harder to get away with repeating brazen lies without paying a price…"*

Yeah, Arianna, you nailed that one.

What was promised to be an information superhighway too often seems to be a dirt road of stupidity, pornography, narcissism, fraud, bullying and disinformation. The only saving grace is blogs.

Yes, that's a joke.

In fact, we are currently living in a business environment in which the consolidation of economic power into the hands of a few massive entities is unprecedented.

Google and Facebook completely dominate the internet. There has never been a duopoly that so dominated a medium. And was so free of governmental restraint. Or self-restraint, for that matter.

They are not just selling media space like the TV, radio, and print people are. They are weaving their way into the fabric of the world's leading companies.

According to *Ad Age*, Google and Facebook now have teams of people who are embedded in the marketing departments of over half the world's 50 leading brands. They are not just vendors to these companies, they are part of the process of developing marketing and advertising strategies.

They are so far ahead of the traditional media, they might as well be from another century…oh, wait a minute. They are.

I have often written about the pitiful efforts of traditional media to fight against the tidal wave of online media. They are too timid to address the shortcomings of online media directly.

They have no strategy to defend their businesses – other than whining. These guys can't find their dicks with a flashlight.

But let's stop picking on traditional media for a minute and have a look at how the cozy relationships between Google, Facebook and their marketing partners might be working.

Apparently when it was revealed that Facebook had overstated their viewing times by as much as 80% for two years, P&G and Unilever were bragging that because of their close relationship with Facebook, they were not surprised. The above-mentioned *Ad Age* article says...

> *"P&G and Unilever...weren't blindsided by the recent revelation that Facebook overstated average video view times."*

Really? So here's what I'd like to know:

- If P&G and Unilever knew that Facebook's numbers were bullshit, why didn't they say something?

- Or, why didn't they tell Facebook? Or, did they tell Facebook and Facebook did nothing?

- Or, did they all conspire to keep it quiet and have a good laugh about it?

It has to be one of these.

As we'll see, P&G later paid a high price for their coziness with Facebook.

## I'LL BE WATCHING YOU

In June of 2017 it was revealed that Google is not just following us online, they are also tracking us in the physical world. They are stalking us through our credit card transactions to see when and where we shop and what we are buying. This raises three questions:

- Who gave credit card companies permission to sell our purchasing information to Google?

- Who gave Google the right to that information?

- Who is Google sharing or selling this information to?

As usual, there is probably some language buried deep in the incomprehensible legal jive we agree to when we sign up for a credit card that allows this intrusion into our privacy.

According to *The Washington Post*, Google…

> *"…declined to detail how the new system works or what companies are analyzing records of credit and debit cards on Google's behalf….Marc Rotenberg, executive director of the Electronic Privacy Information Center said, 'What's really fascinating to me is that as the companies become increasingly intrusive in terms of their data collection, they also become more secretive.'"*

Meanwhile Amazon, Google, Apple and other tech giants are now capable of listening to virtually anything said in our homes.

If you have an Amazon Echo, a Google Home or an Apple Home-Pod they are constantly monitoring conversations within their range. Once you say the magic word they begin recording what is said.

What happens to those recordings? Who the hell knows.

Walt Mossberg has been one of the most articulate and influential writers about technology for over two decades. He retired in 2017. In his last column, he wrote...

> *"...we need much, much stronger standards for security and privacy than now exist... it's time to stop dancing around the privacy and security issues and pass real, binding laws."*

## TURNING AD DOLLARS INTO PENNIES

Now we're going to follow the money and watch as the amazing world of ad tech magically turns a dollar of online display advertising into 3¢ of value. One word of caution — copywriter math is a notoriously dicey enterprise. Please take the following as "directional" rather than literal.

Kindly step into my lab...

First we start with a dollar. We give it to our media agency to buy some display advertising for us

According to the *World Federation of Advertisers* (WFA) here's what happens next:

- First, your media agency takes about 5¢ in service fees.
- Then their Trading Desk takes about 15¢.
- Then their *Demand Side Platform* (DSP) takes about 10¢.
- Next, some other ad tech middlemen take about 25¢ for targeting, data, and verification.
- Then an *Ad Exchange* takes about 5¢. This excerpted section of the chart we saw earlier sums it up nicely.

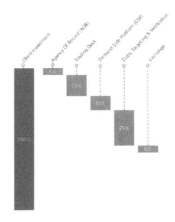

So before an ad appears, 60¢ of your dollar has already been spent on ...something. I don't know what, I guess "technology" or "process" or something equally vague.

All these middlemen say that they add value to your media buy by precision targeting your ad at your perfect customer, in the perfect location, with the perfect message at the perfect time. Which results in an average click rate of 6 clicks per 10,000 ads. One can only imagine the results if the customer, location, message, and timing were not perfect.

On the other hand, Proctor & Gamble, the world's largest advertiser, says that all the techno-precision targeting actually got them *fewer* customers. More about this later.

Well, the good news is, you still have 40¢ left.

But the problem is, you can't get 40¢ worth of advertising for your 40¢. You see, according to *The New York Times, Digiday* and other reliable people, only about 50% of online ads are "viewable." This is because online ads often don't load in time for a person to see them. Or they appear "below the fold" where they are not visible. Or a fraudster sends a pixel that says it's an ad or software engineers at the publisher stuff one pixel into the frame which reads as an ad. Or ads are stacked behind one another where they can't be seen (it's a nasty game, this.)

So sadly, we're now going to have to mark your 40¢ down by 50% to 20¢ to account for the "viewability" problem. Of course, your agency will show you metrics that prove that the viewability problem doesn't apply to *you*. Oh no, *your* ads are 100% viewable. It's always *the other guy* who's the sucker. There's some amazing algebra going on here. Every individual advertiser's ads are 100% viewable, but in aggregate they're 50% viewable. Must be a copywriter doing the math.

Now we have 20¢ left

But, darn it, other kinds of fraud also have to be taken into account.

You see, some of your ads are very likely to run on make-believe websites that have make-believe traffic and make-believe clicks. Of course, you didn't ask for that, but that's what you get. The one thing you don't get are make-believe invoices.

Your agency will tell you that they have protection against fraud. They have cyber-security this and 100%-guaranteed-ad fraud-protection that. It's all horseshit. Do some reading.

As we saw earlier, ad fraud is estimated to be between 2% and 90%. In other words, no one has a clue. As we will soon see, no matter what your "cyber-security team" tells you, nobody knows how much fraud there is in online advertising.

Since we accounted for a little ad fraud in our last step, let's be conservative and say that only 10% of your remaining 20¢ will be eaten by fraud. That leaves us with 18¢

Let's recap. So far we've discovered that for our advertising dollar we have probably gotten about 60¢ worth of fees and technology, 20¢ worth of viewability issues, 2¢ worth of additional fraud, and 18¢ worth of viewable real ads.

But our next problem is that display ads have alarmingly low impact. It's called "banner blindness." According to *Lumen*, a research company that measures this stuff, only 2/3 of "viewable" impressions are actually *viewed* by someone. Sorry, that just cost us about six cents.

Well, we're getting down to the end here and we have 12 cents left. There's just one more value killer we have to account for - people.

According to the above-mentioned Lumen group, 75% of the time people don't even spend a *second* looking at online ads. Even the clowns — I mean professionals — at the *Interactive Advertising Bureau* won't accept a digital ad that isn't in view for a second as an "impresssion." This is not helpful to our value calculation. It takes our 12¢ down to 3¢.

So, at the end if the line, it looks like you are probably getting somewhere about 3¢ worth of actual ads seen by actual people for every dollar you spend on display advertising.

I know you may be feeling a little depressed by all the money you've been pissing away. But please, look at the big picture. You're on the web. How cool is that!

## THE BIG DOG BARKS

In July of 2016 the world's largest advertiser, *Procter & Gamble*, told the online media industry, and its lapdogs in the agency industry, that it had had enough and it wasn't gonna take any more.

This came on the heels of another shocker by P&G. Also in July of 2016, P&G announced that it was ending its "precision targeted" ad program with Facebook. It had moved over a third of its advertising spending on line in the previous few years. And in a 12-month period its sales had dropped by 8%, or about six billion dollars.

At the annual "leadership" meeting (I use the quotes advisedly) of the *Interactive Advertising Bureau*, Marc Pritchard, chief brand officer for P&G, told the assembled squids, slugs, and tap dancers that unless they cleaned up their act and adhered to some specific guidelines he laid down they weren't going to get any more P&G money.

Pritchard called online media practices, *"murky at best and fraudulent at worst."*

That's nothing new to us. But it's a whole different thing when it comes from the world's largest advertiser than when it comes from some dumb-ass blogger.

Of course, the question nobody wants to ask is this: Where have the agencies been who should have been protecting their clients all this time? The kindest explanation is that they've been asleep at the wheel. But, please, don't kid a kidder. How can it be that the people closest to the speakers couldn't hear the music?

There is something about agency silence that is screaming at me. For years we've had a steady stream of scandalous news about online advertising. There have been dozens of stories about corruption, click fraud, traffic fraud, misrepresentation of data, bots, plots and what-nots. And not a single one of the revelations has come from inside an advertising agency. Not one. You've got to ask yourself why?

If agencies are supposed to be the experts on the effective use of media dollars, how can it be that they were the last to know about all these problems? Is it possible? Does it even pass the smell test?

The answer is no. The most likely scenario is that they've known what's going on and have been playing a double game. I believe agency leaders have been hiding the ugly details from their clients behind an impenetrable smokescreen of "big data" horseshit.

Online advertising has two very compelling advantages for agencies: it is lucrative and largely incomprehensible. Most clients, even the most sophisticated, think they know what's going on. But they don't.

Pritchard said

> "We serve ads to consumers through a non-transparent media supply chain with spotty compliance to common standards, unreliable measurement, hidden rebates and new inventions like bot and methbot fraud…"

The ad industry spent several decades developing common standards for measurement, standard definitions for transparency, and standard practices for third party verification. But in recent years it has thrown these standards away like infatuated schoolgirls mesmerized by a bunch of fast-talking techno-hustlers who came swaggering into town to blind them with pseudo-science.

For example, AdNews reported that "the 'viewability scores' for Facebook video ads are as low as 2% when compared with the standard used for TV ads."

The ad industry and its clients have demonstrated a degree of gullibility that is beyond explanation.

Will the advertising and marketing industries join P&G and insist on standards of transparency or will they cave and let the cuties of the online media industry continue to bamboozle them? That's the big question.

The big dog has barked. Let's see what the silly poodles do.

# Chapter Three:

## What To Do

On May 24, 2017, the Association of National Advertisers and its cyber-security consultants White Ops announced that based on a study they had conducted, online ad fraud would drop by 10% in 2017.

The ceo of the ANA said, "Marketers worldwide are successfully adopting strategies and tactics to fight digital ad fraud." High fives all around. Except for a few little things…

One week later, Check Point, a software technology company, announced a previously undetected fraud operation called "Fireball." Forbes said it "might be the biggest Android ad fraud ever."

Check Point reported that Fireball had infected 250 million computers and 20% of corporate networks worldwide.

Dr. Augustine Fou, mentioned earlier, has a PhD from MIT, teaches digital and integrated marketing at Rutgers and NYU, and was SVP, digital strategy lead, at McCann/MRM Worldwide. He is one of the world's leading authorities on ad fraud. Dr. Fou calculated that Fireball could generate 30 billion fraudulent ad impressions a minute. That's not a typo — 30 billion a minute. He called it "fraud on such a massive scale it is beyond belief."

And who's buying all these fraudulent ad impressions? The same suckers who think "Marketers worldwide are successfully adopting strategies and tactics to fight digital ad fraud."

## THE COALITION TO DO NOTHING

In April of 2017, alarmed by a tidal wave of consumer antipathy to the awfulness of online advertising, a group of big-time advertisers, publishers, agencies, and media announced a coalition to "rid the internet of annoying ads."

According to *MarketingWeek*...

> *"The 'Coalition for Better Ads' aims to take on the "Herculanean task" of bringing together advertisers, agencies, ad tech and publishers to come up with global standards on digital advertising to tackle the rise of ad blocking."*

I'm pretty sure they mean "Herculean" but, hey, who cares about language anymore?

Here are the goals of this coalition:

- *Create consumer-based, data-driven standards that companies in the online advertising industry can use to improve the consumer ad experience*
- *In conjunction with the IAB Tech Lab, develop and deploy technology to implement these standards*
- *Encourage awareness of the standards among consumers and businesses in order to ensure wide uptake and elicit feedback*

This reminds me of an initiative announced over 5 years ago by the IAB called *"Making Measurement Make Sense"* in which they formed a "coalition" to try to make sense of all the incomprehensible metrics the online industry was peddling. At the time I wrote...

> *"The enormous success of digital advertising is based on the fortunate*

*circumstance that almost no one understands anything about the numbers."*

Happily for the online ad industry the "coalition" came to nothing and the confusion over online ad metrics is greater than ever. And the greater the confusion, the bigger the payday.

This new *"Coalition For Better Ads"* (CBA) is doomed to spin in circles and accomplish half-measures because it *will not deal* with the real problem.

Instead, Google, who is the big dog in this coalition, has announced that they will decide what consumers want to see by building a limited ad blocker into their Chrome browser. This blocker will eliminate pop-ups, auto-play videos and certain type of full-page interstitials (ads that get in-between you and the website you're trying to connect with.) But surprise!…they'll allow the ads they sell on their DoubleClick platform. So what we have here is Dracula guarding the blood bank.

Some people, including yours truly, think this could lead to legal troubles for Google. Here's what the *Electronic Frontier Foundation* (EFF) had to say…

> *"…While we welcome the willingness to tackle annoying ads, the CBA's criteria do not address a key reason many of us install ad blockers: to protect ourselves against the non-consensual tracking and surveillance that permeates the advertising ecosystem operated by the members of the CBA."*

If the CBA just got rid of *tracking*, a great many of the problems consumers, publishers, and advertisers are facing would evaporate.

- Consumers would not be constantly stalked and harassed by tracking software leading to insufferable "precision targeted" ads.
- Quality publishers would be able to monetize their audiences instead of having the audience stolen by crappy or imaginary sites through "data-leakage" and re-targeting.

• Advertisers would know who they are reaching and where; they would not have most of their media dollars pissed away on ad tech middlemen; they would not have to rely on problematic ad networks.

But this coalition will deal with *everything but the problem*. The reason they will not deal with the real problem is that the people who own the internet – Google and Facebook and Amazon – will never allow it. Tracking is essential to them.

The duopoly of Google and Facebook (which I like to call Goobook) don't just dominate web advertising, they essentially own it. Here are some remarkable facts:

- Google's market share in the U.S. is 87%. In Europe it is 91%..

- Facebook and the other social media companies it owns (What's App, Instagram, and Facebook Messenger) have a 75% share.

- According to Pivotal Research Group, in the third quarter of 2016, 99% of all new online ad revenue went to Goobook.

- The US online ad industry grew 22% in 2016. But outside of the duopoly the growth rate was about 0.

- Goobook now account for 77% of all online ad revenue in the US. Outside of China, their next closest rival has less than a 3% share.

It is beyond mind-blowing to think that there are about 1.2 *billion* websites in the world and 2 of them are raking in 77% of U.S. ad revenue. Imagine if Channel 6 in Boise and Channel 9 in Waco were recipients of 77% of all TV revenue in the US. Except there aren't 1.2 billion TV channels. The Goobook duopoly is *thousands of times more concentrated.*

In contrast to Google, in recent days Apple has also announced an initiative to deal with the public's disgust at online advertising.

Apple's solution is far better.

Apple's Safari browser will soon employ "Intelligent Tracking Prevention." This will keep marketers from tracking us across sites. Don Marti sums up the benefit of Safari's solution succinctly:

- Nifty machine learning technology is coming in on the user's side.

- "Legitimate" uses do not include cross-site tracking.

- Safari's protection is automatic and client-side, so no blocklist politics.

The key difference in the way Apple and Google approach the problem can be found in the nature of the companies. Apple makes very little money from online advertising and has a self-interest in defending their users' experiences.

Google, on the other hand, makes virtually all of its money from advertising and has a self-interest in protecting tracking and surveillance marketing. The key thing to remember is that most of the major players in online advertising have a big stake in surveillance marketing. They will fight like hell to protect tracking.

It is not surprising that Google's "Better Ads" solution would look like it's treating the disease while actually only treating symptoms.

## WRONG PROBLEM, WRONG SOLUTION

Recently, in one of the great insights of the 21st century, a member of a panel at the Cannes Festival of ~~Insane Advertising Excess~~ Creativity had this to say about ad blocking…

> *"The root cause of digital ad blocking is digital ads."*

No shit? Imagine the poor bastards who traveled 5,000 miles, paid $1,200 a night for a room, and $25 a glass for putrid rosé who had to listen to this twaddle.

By the way, it wasn't some content strategy dipshit from Brooklyn who made this brilliant statement. It was the ceo of *The New York Times*. No, you cannot make this up.

The panel in question consisted of the following: the above-mentioned ceo of *The Times*, the ceo of the *Interactive Advertising Bureau*, and a "content strategist" (yeah, probably a dipshit from Brooklyn.) The panel was called, *"Block You: Why World Class Creativity Will Obliterate Ad Blocking."*

As you can see, the theme of the panel was how to overcome the problem of ad blocking. Maybe I'm a little slow, but it seems to me that there are about 1,000 people on the planet to whom ad blocking is a *problem* and about 7 billion to whom it's a *solution*.

As usual, the view from inside the beltway was completely ass-backwards. Their solutions went something like this:

1. *The creative work needs to be "world class."* These guys really need to get their heads out of their asses and take a look at what's going on. *World* class? This crap isn't even *gym* class. Tracking has made the web a direct response medium and in direct response the creative work *never* gets better. Never.

2. *The big bad ad blocking companies need to stop "profiteering."*

Likewise, not gonna happen. The culture of the web demands that anyone who can make a buck does so. Sure, some ad blocking entrepreneurs are shaking down marketers. Are we supposed to be shocked that there is sleaze in the online ad culture?

3. *Collaboration.* Everyone has to get together, hold hands, and put aside their self-interest in the furtherance of a good user experience. Yeah, any minute now.

There is only one solution to the problem. Take away surveillance and online advertising will become a minor annoyance like all other advertising forms instead of an intolerable, disreputable scourge.

## AD BLOCKERS ARE NOT THE ANSWER

I'm uncomfortable with the idea of ad blockers. As an unrepentant ad person, I don't like the idea. And yet I use ad blockers.

According to *PageFair* there are now over 600 million connected devices in the world sporting ad blockers. In the US, it is estimated that about 25% of desktop computers are now using ad blockers. And, as noted above, Google is adding a partial ad blocking option to its Chrome browser - the most used browser in the world.

For now, the most popular defense against obnoxious online advertising is ad blocking. But ad blocking is a blunt instrument that has the potential to do serious damage to aspects of the web we all enjoy.

Like it or not, advertising funds just about everything on the web we like. Without advertising you'd be stuck with nothing but blogs and porn. And blogs are no fun at all.

It would be nice to believe that people would be willing to pay for things they enjoy online but most experiments in "paywall" web publishing have been a failure.

So the question becomes, how can we encourage an acceptable version of online advertising that will allow us to enjoy the things we like about the web without the insufferable annoyance of the current online ad model?

The solution is not that complicated. The invisible hand that powers just about everything we hate about online advertising is tracking. There is no reason why online advertising can't be more acceptable and the model of ad tech reformed if we just get rid of tracking.

This will require changes in the web browsers we use. Average people do not have the technical knowledge to create their own browsers or run a data center. We need to be able to tell our web browsers:

1. Give me an easy way to prevent my activity on one site from being used to target me on another site.

2. As the surveillance marketers find new ways to stalk me, keep
   up with them and apply my choices to the new tracking
   schemes.

Online advertisers would then not be able to stalk us everywhere
we went on the web; fake news would be less likely to draw "program-
matically" delivered advertising money; quality publishers would have
a better chance at survival; the economic incentive for click bait would
diminish, and many other undesirable aspects of web advertising would
be greatly minimized.

We could enjoy what we like about the web without having to
resort to the heavy hand of ad blockers.

## WHAT IS THE ANSWER FOR ADVERTISERS?

Taking a global view, the whole question of the effectiveness of online advertising is up for grabs.

In July of 2017, Procter & Gamble announced that it had eliminated about $140 million of online display advertising from its most recent advertising effort and saw no ill effect.

According to *The Wall Street Journal*... P&G's scrapping of this advertising *"had little impact on its business, proving that those digital ads were largely ineffective."*

But let's say you don't agree and are convinced that digital advertising is effective for you. The allure of lower digital CPMs (costs-per-thousand) and the mirage of "precision targeting" are the most treacherous pitfalls for you.

While low CPMs are considered a key performance index by some marketers, they are often exactly the opposite.

The relationship between lower CPMs and worthless inventory is very clear. The lower your CPMs the higher the likelihood is that you are buying:

- Bots instead of people
- Unsafe inventory on questionable sites
- Sourced traffic

The key to better ad performance is to stay as far away as possible from questionable ad exchanges and the ad tech industry's programmatic snake pit. Avoiding the ad tech industry is not only good policy, it is also good business.

As we saw earlier, a significant component of advertising dollars are skimmed by the ad tech supply chain. The ad tech supply chain is supposed to produce "precision targeting" which is purported to increase the productivity of your ad dollars. In fact, according to a study by Dr. Augustine Fou, it does exactly the opposite.

According to Dr. Fou, buying *directly* from quality publishers increases the productivity of display advertising by at least seven times and perhaps as much as 27 times compared to buying through a programmatic exchange.

The search for the precision targeted city of gold actually seems to diminish display ad dollar productivity.

If Dr. Fou is correct, the value proposition of ad tech is completely backwards. Programmatic buying is not more efficient, it is less efficient.

The CEO of the Association of National Advertisers has said *"marketers have to take their industry back."* I couldn't agree more.

When I think about how online advertisers are being penetrated in every possible orifice I wonder why in the world they don't do something about it?

Let's sum up and see if you agree with my logic. Ad tech is stealing your money, threatening your security, and alienating your customers.

- If you're an advertiser, adtech middlemen are scraping 40-70% of your media dollars.

- P&G says that "precision targeting," the great value proposition of ad tech was actually harmful to their marketing efforts.

- Because adtech is a black box, you don't know where your ads run or who may be profiting from them. In fact, you may be unwittingly funding terrorists, nazis, and pornographers.

- Adtech helps fraudsters steal...who knows?... anywhere from 2% to 90% of your media budget.

- This is why 70% of marketing executives say they are dissatisfied with the state of online advertising.

- 90% of marketers say they are planning to review their programmatic contracts in 2017 to get more transparency. Ad tech is the mortal enemy of transparency.

- If you're a quality online publisher, ad tech is stealing money from you by following your valuable audience to the crappiest website they can be found on, and serving them ads there instead of on your site.

- If you're an advertiser, this means ad tech is essentially following your customer to the bathroom in the basement of the luxury mall and trying to sell her your necklaces there (h/t Tom Goodwin.)

- If you're an online publisher, adtech sees to it that you are constantly struggling to monetize your content while the duopoly (Google and Facebook) that create *no content* reap 77% of all online ad revenue (outside China) and the valuable audience you are spending money to develop is being stolen from you by your least reputable rivals through data leakage.

If Dr. Fou's research is correct, the promise of ad tech - making your online ad dollar more productive - is actually wrong, and it makes it less productive.

So, Ms Advertiser, why don't you insist on a simple transparent buying process in which your agency buys directly from online publishers?

You'll know exactly where your advertising is running, exactly whom you're buying from, exactly what you're paying, and exactly what you're getting. And your online ad dollar will go further.

In what universe is the corrupt, incomprehensible, wasteful and dangerous world of ad tech better than that?

## WHAT IS THE ANSWER FOR CONSUMERS?

There is a saying in web world — if you're not paying for the product, you *are* the product.

What this means is that the people who are providing you with "free" online products and services are leveraging your personal information to make money off you.

As far as I'm concerned, there's nothing wrong with that as long as you are aware of it and have agreed to it - which most people are not and have not.

Tracking as it is currently practiced is on its way to extinction in Europe. The EU will be implementing something called the GDPR next year. This will make it mandatory for online entities to get consumers' prior permission before they collect, share, or sell personal information. This is a big step forward.

However, here in the States, and elsewhere in the world, we are still in the dark ages.

There are a few simple things average people can do to give themselves some degree of protection. First, a little philosophy

In some cases, you might want to grant a website the ability to recognize you. For example, you may not want to have to sign in to Facebook every time you go there. You may not want to have to enter all your credit card information every time you order something from Amazon. In which case, you might want to allow them to drop "first party" cookies on you. A cookie is a software thread that can be used to identify you.

However, you may *not* want to grant them the right to drop cookies on you that follow you to other websites, or allow them to drop cookies on you from unknown third parties, or sell the information they have about you to data brokers or other online entities.

There are two free programs that seem to be the best at allowing you to choose what kind of trackers you are willing to live with and what kind you can't. They are called *Privacy Badger* (created by the

*Electronic Frontier Foundation*) and *Disconnect*. I suggest you take a few minutes to explore each of these and decide which is easier for you to understand and operate.

Also, there are search engines like *DuckDuckGo* that do not track you. Among major browsers, Apple's Safari is best at protecting you from being tracked from site to site, even in different tabs of the same browsing session. Firefox is working on it.

By limiting the ability of advertisers to track you, over time these programs should have the additional benefit of eliminating some of the creepier advertisers that are stalking you.

There are also organizations like the Electronic Frontier Foundation and others that are fighting for consumer privacy. You might want to support them.

In the long run, we need to switch the power relationship away from those who monetize the web, toward those who utilize it. It's not going to be easy.

Jeremiah Grossman, is the founder of WhiteHat Security, a web security firm. Mr. Grossman says, *"We're talking megabillion-dollar industries totally designed to track you online,…That's their mission in life."*

Limiting tracking would require some simple, reasonable legislation. The legislation should codify three ideas based on the following principle — individuals have a right to know and limit those who are collecting and utilizing personal information about them.

1. An individual's permission must be received before an online entity can collect private personal information about her.

2. An individual's permission must be received before a 3rd party can collect private personal information about her.

3. An individual's permission must be received before her private personal information is shared or sold to anyone.

These principles seem perfectly sensible and reasonable. And yet, they are poison to the surveillance marketing industry.

We are being held hostage to some very large entities: Google, Facebook, Amazon, the Interactive Advertising Bureau, the 4A's, the Association of National Advertisers, and others.

These people are now in the surveillance business. They are the power behind ad tech, tracking, and surveillance marketing. Their business is collecting, selling, and exploiting the details of our personal lives and our personal behavior.

It's bad business.

*A guy name Kyle Zak is suing the Bose Corp.*

*Zak claims a Bose app that is downloaded by customers to activate their wireless headphones secretly tracks their listening habits and sells the information to third parties.*

*Whether Bose is guilty is something for the courts to decide. But this lawsuit highlights a very important issue for us – when do we say enough-is-enough to surveillance marketing?*

*Who in their right mind would ever suspect that their headphones were spying on them?*

*But we have reached a point of crisis in "mar tech" (marketing technology) and "ad tech" (advertising technology.) There are so many things keeping track of our activities (our phones, our thermostats, every website we visit, every link we click, our Siris and Alexas) it's impossible to know how much information about us is being collected, stolen, or sold on the open market.*

*If you're not paranoid you're not paying attention.*

## Acknowledgements

An enormous amount of gratitude is owed to several people.

First to Barbara Lippert who convinced me to write this book when I was planning to write a different one. Several people did me the great service of reading the book or reviewing ideas about the book and giving me valuable comments: Barbara, Philip Mezey, Claudia Caplan, Maria Winston, Lucy Hoffman, Jay Tannenbaum, Sharon Krinsky, Rich Siegel, George Tannenbaum, and some others who I'm sure I'm forgetting.

I owe a lot to Doc Searls, Shailin Dhar, and Dr. Augustine Fou whose writing and knowledge of the problems of online surveillance informed every page of this book. I owe a special thanks to Don Marti whose brilliance helped me through some technical issues far above the pay grade of a dumb-ass blogger.

Once again, I have to thank the wonderful Bonnie Miguel for overseeing the design and production of the book.

I also want to thank the people who regularly read my blog and newsletter. They give me the (perhaps illusory) belief that I'm not just talking to myself.

## About The Author

Bob Hoffman is a best-selling author, speaker, and advisor. He is one of the most sought-after international speakers on advertising and marketing.

Bob has written two successful books including *"Marketers Are From Mars, Consumers Are From New Jersey"* which Amazon chose as *"#1 Hot Prospect"* in advertising, and *"101 Contrarian Ideas About Advertising"* which became Amazon's #1 selling advertising book .

He is author of the popular *"Ad Contrarian"* blog, named one of the world's most influential marketing and advertising blogs by *Business Insider.*

Bob has been the ceo of two independent agencies and the US operation of an international agency. He has created advertising for *McDonald's, Toyota, Pepsico, Bank of America, AT&T* and more companies than he cares to think about. Through his company, *Type A Group,* Bob advises advertisers, agencies, and media.

In 2012 he was selected *Ad Person of the Year* by the San Francisco Advertising Club.

Bob has served on the boards of the *Advertising and Marketing International Network, the Foundation for Osteoporosis Research and Education,* and spent one year as Special Assistant to the Executive Director of the *California Academy of Sciences.*

Printed in Great Britain
by Amazon